KT-163-345

Marvellous Maths
Division

By David L. Stienecker

Illustrations by Richard Maccabe

CHERRYTREE BOOKS

A Cherrytree Book

Adapted by A S Publishing from
Discovering Math
First published by Benchmark Books
Copyright © Marshall Cavendish Corporation 1996
Series created by Blackbirch Graphics Inc
Series editor: Tanya Lee Stone

This edition first published in 1997
by Cherrytree Press Ltd
a subsidiary of
The Chivers Company Ltd
Windsor Bridge Road
Bath BA2 3AX

British Library Cataloguing in Publication Data
Stienecker, David L.
    Division
    1. Division—Juvenile literature 2. Division—Problems,
exercises, etc.—Juvenile literature
    I. Title
    372.7'2

ISBN 0 7451 5311 9

Printed and bound in the USA

Contents

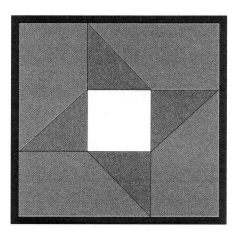

The Friendship Star

Ever heard of a friendship star? This is what it looks like. The pattern is made from triangles.

- How many triangles are used to make the star?

- How many stars could you make with fifteen triangles? Would you have any triangles left over? How could you find out?

- To check your answer, make fifteen triangles like this one. Use them to make friendship stars.

If you know how many in each group, you can divide to find how many groups.

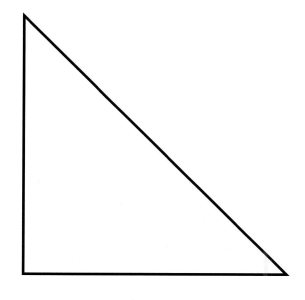

Friendship stars are used as a pattern in some patchwork quilts. Patchwork quilts are a kind of blanket. They are made by sewing small pieces of cloth together. That's why they are called 'patchwork'.

Here is what a patchwork quilt made with friendship stars might look like.

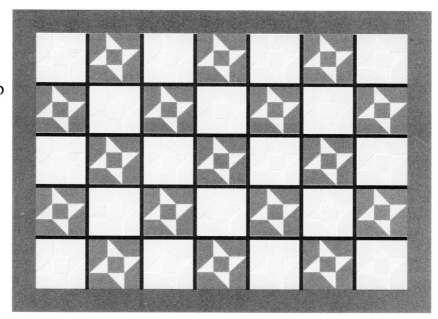

• There are 140 triangles in this quilt. How many friendship stars are there? Use division to find the answer.

• Now suppose you want to use a star like this one to make a quilt. If you have 140 triangles, how many stars like this can you make? Will there be any triangles left over?

Facts Five

This game is played just like bingo. Any number of people can play. One person will have to be chosen as the caller.

Each player will need:

25 playing pieces
or 'markers'

paper and pencil

Get each player to draw a game board like this one on a sheet of paper. Do not write in the book.

F	A	C	T	S
?	?	?	?	?
?	?	?	?	?
?	?	?	?	?
?	?	?	?	?
?	?	?	?	?

Then each player writes a number from 1 to 9 in each of the boxes on his or her game board, like this:

F	A	C	T	S
3	7	4	3	6
5	8	4	2	9
9	7	1	4	3
6	4	5	1	2
8	3	4	9	3

How to play:

• The caller calls out a division problem. For example, 'Under A, how many 4's in 20', or 'Under S, what is 12 divided by 3'. The caller should write down all of the calls he or she makes.

• The players who have the number that solves the division problem should cover the number with a marker.

• The first player to cover all the numbers in a row, column or diagonal calls out 'Facts' and wins the game.

• The caller uses his or her record of calls to check the winner's card.

• For a new game, use the same card, make new ones or exchange cards.

Some division problems don't work out exactly; the number left over is called a remainder.

Dividing by Subtracting

Division is just another way of subtracting the same number over and over again. You can see how this works by using a calculator.

To find 30 ÷ 6, count how many 6's can be subtracted from 30, like this:

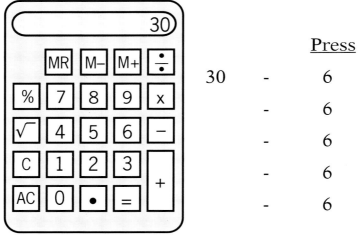

		Press		You See
30	-	6	=	**24**
	-	6	=	**18**
	-	6	=	**12**
	-	6	=	**6**
	-	6	=	**0**

• How many 6's were subtracted from 30?

• Use a calculator to do a little division by subtraction. Try it with these division problems. Some of them will have remainders. When you are finished, try some problems of your own.

36 ÷ 6	49 ÷ 7	28 ÷ 4	27 ÷ 3	64 ÷ 8
45 ÷ 5	36 ÷ 9	46 ÷ 7	54 ÷ 6	72 ÷ 9
36 ÷ 4	49 ÷ 8	35 ÷ 5	63 ÷ 9	58 ÷ 7
75 ÷ 6	95 ÷ 5	37 ÷ 4	57 ÷ 9	49 ÷ 5

Dividing by 9's and 3's

It's easy to tell if a number can be evenly divided by 9. All you have to do is add the number's digits. If the sum is more than one digit, add up the digits again.

Continue in this way until you have only one digit left. If the digit is 9, then the original number can be divided by 9. Here's an example:

- Can 468 be evenly divided by 9?

  Add the digits. $\boxed{4 + 6 + 8 = 18}$

  Add again. $\boxed{1 + 8 = 9}$

    The single-digit sum is 9. So 468 is divisible by 9.

You can use the same method to find out if a number can be exactly divided by 3. If the single-digit sum is 3, 6 or 9, then the original number is divisible by 3.

- Can 348 be evenly divided by 3?

  Add the digits. $\boxed{3 + 4 + 8 = 15}$

  Add again. $\boxed{1 + 5 = 6}$

    The single-digit is 6. So 348 is divisible by 3.

- Use this method to find out which of these numbers can be evenly divided by 3 and 9.

  765   267   376   558   2,126   1,362   4,063

  1,125   11,574   59,239   2,886   22,359

Beanstalk Race

Have you ever heard the story of Jack and the beanstalk? Jack climbs a really tall beanstalk to look for a goose that lays golden eggs. But when he gets to the top he runs into a giant and barely escapes with his skin.

Here's a beanstalk game to play. The object is to see who can get to the top leaf first.

You will need:

• Two different markers. Coins or buttons, or anything small will do.

• Paper and pencil and a pack of division cards. To make the cards, write each of these division problems on a piece of card.

14 ÷ 7	20 ÷ 5	36 ÷ 6	16 ÷ 2	55 ÷ 9	24 ÷ 7
43 ÷ 6	64 ÷ 9	74 ÷ 8	83 ÷ 9	33 ÷ 4	50 ÷ 8
14 ÷ 3	27 ÷ 8	48 ÷ 9	59 ÷ 7	19 ÷ 4	20 ÷ 3

How to play:

• Turn the cards face down and shuffle them.

• Each player draws a card in turn, solves the problem and returns the card to the pile.

• If the division problem has a remainder, move up that number of leaves. Land on the same leaf as your opponent, and he or she must move down two leaves. If you solve a problem with no remainder, move down two leaves.

Cross Numbers

This game is like a crossword puzzle with numbers. The clues are division problems. The answers are the quotients.

Copy or trace the puzzle on to a sheet of paper. Then give it a try.

The answer to a division problem is called a quotient.

Across

(2) 2)66

(4) 4)604

(7) 6)192

(9) 3)171

(11) 12)300

(12) 10)910

(14) 12)504

(16) 8)608

(18) 3)258

(20) 15)345

(22) 21)252

(24) 7)574

(25) 9)747

(27) 11)352

(29) 6)792

1. ?	?	2. ?	3. ?	?	4. ?	5. ?	6. ?
7. ?	8. ?	?	9. ?	10. ?	?	11. ?	?
?	12. ?	13. ?	?	14. ?	15. ?	?	?
?	?	16. ?	17. ?	?	18. ?	19. ?	?
20. ?	21. ?	?	22. ?	23. ?	?	24. ?	?
?	25. ?	26. ?	?	27. ?	28. ?	?	?
?	?	?	?	?	29. ?	?	?

Down

(1) 4)92

(3) 5)175

(5) 3)156

(6) 12)180

(8) 10)290

(10) 13)962

(13) 8)136

(15) 30)840

(17) 13)793

(19) 9)612

(21) 22)836

(23) 42)966

(26) 21)672

(28) 19)399

11

Remainder Riddle

Most of the division problems in this table work exactly. But some have remainders. Make a copy of the table. Shade in all the boxes with remainders and you'll have the answer to this riddle:

How can you spell mousetrap with three letters?

3 ÷ 2	5 ÷ 2	7 ÷ 2	8 ÷ 2	11 ÷ 2	13 ÷ 2	15 ÷ 2
17 ÷ 2	18 ÷ 2	3 ÷ 3	6 ÷ 3	11 ÷ 3	12 ÷ 3	17 ÷ 3
19 ÷ 3	21 ÷ 3	24 ÷ 3	27 ÷ 3	6 ÷ 4	9 ÷ 4	14 ÷ 4
18 ÷ 4	20 ÷ 4	24 ÷ 4	28 ÷ 4	33 ÷ 4	36 ÷ 4	7 ÷ 5
13 ÷ 5	16 ÷ 5	22 ÷ 5	25 ÷ 5	31 ÷ 5	35 ÷ 5	42 ÷ 5
45 ÷ 5	6 ÷ 6	15 ÷ 6	19 ÷ 6	28 ÷ 6	30 ÷ 6	36 ÷ 6
42 ÷ 6	48 ÷ 6	56 ÷ 6	9 ÷ 7	17 ÷ 7	21 ÷ 7	28 ÷ 7
35 ÷ 7	42 ÷ 7	49 ÷ 7	59 ÷ 7	63 ÷ 7	8 ÷ 8	16 ÷ 8
24 ÷ 8	32 ÷ 8	40 ÷ 8	49 ÷ 8	56 ÷ 8	64 ÷ 8	72 ÷ 8
18 ÷ 9	27 ÷ 9	36 ÷ 9	57 ÷ 9	63 ÷ 9	72 ÷ 9	81 ÷ 9

- Now that you know the answer to the riddle, try making some remainder riddle puzzles of your own. Give them to friends to solve.

Mystery Square

The mystery square below holds an interesting secret. To unlock the secret, you'll need to do a little division.

First trace or make a copy of the mystery square, but leave out the division problems.

12)52̄	10)69̄	17)53̄
19)79̄	13)96̄	15)157̄
18)116̄	22)441̄	11)358̄

Now solve the division problems in each box. Each one will have a remainder. Write the remainder in its box in your mystery square.

When your mystery square is finished, add up each row, column and diagonal. The secret is in the answers. Did you discover it?

Greatest Quotient Game

Here's a division game you can play with any number of people. These are the things you will need:

a pack of playing cards

paper and pencil for each player

Prepare the pack of cards by taking out all the picture cards and ten cards. Let the aces stand for 1's and the jokers stand for 0's.

Get each player to draw a game board like this on a sheet of paper.

How to play:

1. Shuffle the cards and lay them face down.

2. In turn, each player takes a card and reads the number aloud. Remember aces are 1's and jokers are 0's.

3. Each player writes the number in any of the boxes on his or her game board. Here's what one player's game board might look like after a 3 and an 8 card have been drawn.

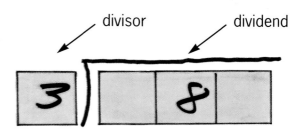

4. After four cards have been drawn, each player's board will have a one-digit divisor and a three-digit dividend. This is how a game board might look at this stage of the game.

5. Each player should solve his or her division problem. The winner is the one with the greatest quotient. What is the quotient of the above game board?

• Try this variation on the game. After everyone has solved their problems, give them 60 seconds to rearrange their digits to try to make a larger quotient. What's the secret?

• Here are some other ways to play the game. Get players to add another digit to the divisor or to the dividend. Draw five cards instead of four.

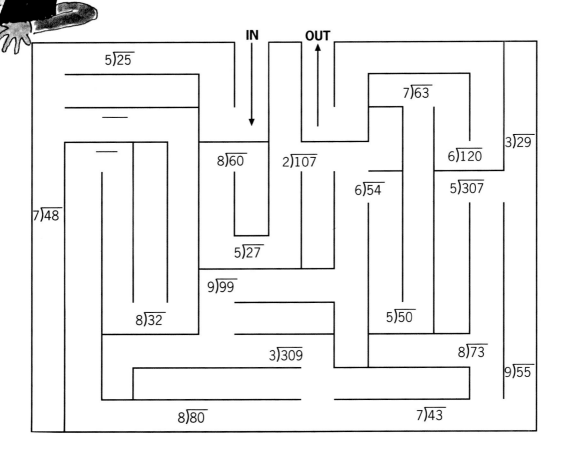

The Path of No Remainders

It's easy to get through this maze if you know how to divide. Just solve the problems and follow the path of no remainders. Use your head not your calculator!

Make a division maze of your own. Show the way out with problems that have no remainders. Or, do it the other way around. Give your maze to a friend. See how quickly your friend can divide.

Missing Numbers Puzzles

Here are some puzzles that will test your thinking skills. Solve them by yourself or with the help of a clever friend.

Try to figure out the missing numbers in these division problems.

It's not as hard as it looks!

```
    2?           ??           1?            1?
  ?)9?         3)8?         6)??          ?)?1
    8            6            ?             7
   16           ??           24           ??
   ??           ?7           ??           2?
    0            0            0            0
```

Now try these.

```
    3?              1??             ???
 ??)? ??          ?)?8?          7)???
   36               5               7
   38              18              25
   ??              ??              ??
    ?              35              ??
                   ??              49
                    ?               ?
```

• Try making up some missing number puzzles of your own. Making them is as much of a challenge as solving them.

Pyramid Puzzles

Here are some pyramid puzzles to improve your division skills. Here's the key to the puzzles:

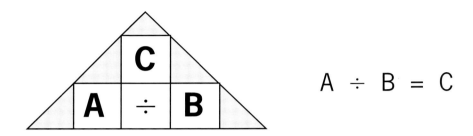

$$A \div B = C$$

Here's an example:

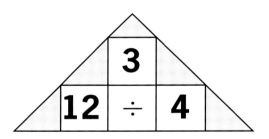

Here are a couple of simple puzzles to get you started.

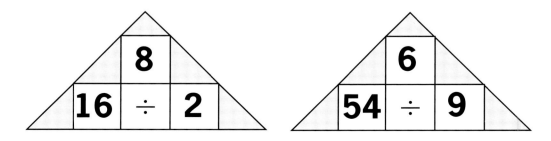

These puzzles are a little bit harder. Remember the pyramid pattern as you solve them. Refer to the key if you get confused.

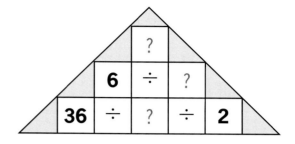

This one will really tug at your brain. Give it a try!

Making the pyramid puzzles is as much of a puzzle as the puzzles themselves. Try making a few and giving them to friends to solve.

A Visit to an Enchanted Forest

Play this game with a friend and work your way through the enchanted forest. Use coins or buttons for markers. Throw a die (one of a pair of dice) to see how many spaces to move. Or, make six number cards. Draw and replace a card during each turn. Always mix the cards up between turns.

How to play:

1. The first player throws the die, then moves that number of spaces. You should count the 'Start' square.

2. If you land on a blue square, you don't have to do anything until your next turn. If you land on a division problem square, find the quotient and move your marker to the square where the quotient appears. If you land on a square with words, do what it says.

3. Watch for those short cuts and danger zones! They can make life really easy or really difficult.

4. The first person to get to the end wins!

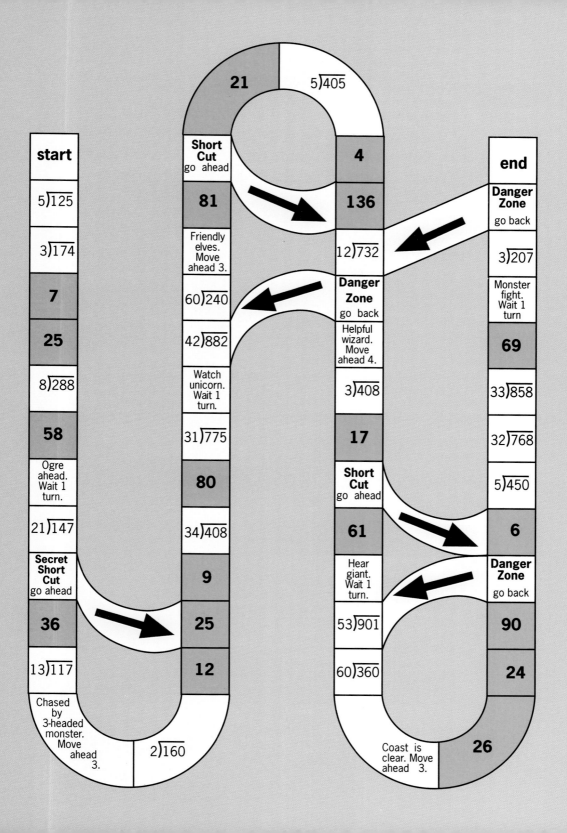

Division Decoder

Use the decoder to find the answers to the riddles below. To decode the decoder just find the quotient for each letter of the alphabet. (Hint: Each quotient has a remainder.)

DECODER

A	B	C	D	E	F	G
$4\overline{)81}$	$18\overline{)39}$	$27\overline{)60}$	$53\overline{)63}$	$35\overline{)74}$	$16\overline{)98}$	$17\overline{)71}$

H	I	J	K	L	M	N
$31\overline{)95}$	$27\overline{)59}$	$2\overline{)163}$	$7\overline{)219}$	$3\overline{)158}$	$5\overline{)409}$	$9\overline{)818}$

O	P	Q	R	S	T	U
$4\overline{)133}$	$6\overline{)435}$	$8\overline{)413}$	$5\overline{)376}$	$7\overline{)509}$	$18\overline{)205}$	$12\overline{)257}$

V	W	X	Y	Z
$13\overline{)135}$	$27\overline{)604}$	$12\overline{)379}$	$13\overline{)125}$	$24\overline{)362}$

What is hard to beat?

20RI   3 R2•20 R1•75 R1•1 R10

2 R3•33 R1•2 R5•52 R2•2 R4•1 R10

2 R4•4 R3•4R3

What kind of insect goes skin diving?

20 R1   81 R4•33 R1•72R5•51 R5•21 R5•

2 R5•11 R7•33 RI

What animal keeps the best time?

20 R1   22 R10•20 R1•11 R7•2 R6•3 R2•

1 R10•33 R1•4 R3

How can a piece of wood become a king?

2 R3•9 R8   2 R3•2 R4•2 R5•90 R8•4 R3

81 R4•20 R1•1 R10•2 R4   2 R5•90 R8•11 R7•33 R1

20 R1   75 R1•21 R5•52 R2•2 R4•75 R1

How can you fall off a ladder without getting hurt?

6 R2•20 R1•52 R2•52 R2   6 R2•75 R1•33 R1•81R4

11 R7•3 R2•2 R4   2 R3•33 R1•11 R7•11 R7•

33 R1•81 R4   75 R1•21 R5•90 R8•4 R3

What happens when a cat eats a lemon?

2 R5•11 R7   2 R3•2 R4•2 R6•33 R1•81 R4•

2 R4•72 R5   20 R1   72 R5•33 R1•21 R5•75 R1

72 R3•21 R5•72 R5•72 R5

• Use the decoder to write some riddles of your own. Better still, have fun and make up your own division code.

23

Dividing with Mayan Numbers

Our System	Mayan System
1	•
2	••
3	•••
4	••••
5	▬
6	•̄
7	••̄
8	•••̄
9	••••̄
10	▬▬
11	•̿
12	••̿
13	•••̿
14	••••̿
15	▬▬▬
16	•̎
17	••̎
18	•••̎
19	••••̎
20	⬯
40	⬯
60	⬯

The Maya were people who lived in Central America long ago. They developed a system of numbers based on only three symbols – a dot, a dash and an oval.

• Solve each of the division problems below. Use the chart to decode the Mayan numbers. Write your answers in Mayan symbols.

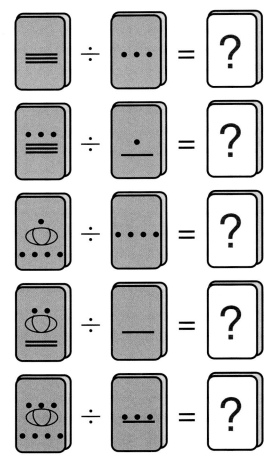

• Use Mayan numbers to make some division problems of your own.

More Riddles and Games

Here are a few more riddles and puzzles to razzle and dazzle you. They all have something to do with division. Give them a try. When you've finished, pass them on to a friend.

Guess the number of zeros in each quotient. Then divide with a calculator to check your guess.

180 ÷ 30   800 ÷ 20

2,800 ÷ 40   6,000 ÷ 50   9,000 ÷ 30

800 ÷ 400   16,000 ÷ 800

40,000 ÷ 80   240,000 ÷ 60

Here are two more puzzles to solve:

The makers of Crunch Crisps had a special offer. Collect 8 labels and get 1 bag free.

Kim persuaded all her friends to give their labels to her. She collected 71 labels in all. How many free bags of Crunch Crisps was Kim able to get?

Two mothers and 2 daughters divided 3 oranges among themselves. Each person received 1 whole orange. How was this possible?

25

Three-Digit Number Puzzle

Select any three-digit number and repeat it to make a six-digit number – for example: 123123. These four things will always be true:

1. Your six-digit number can be equally divided by 13.   **123123 ÷ 13 = 9471**

2. The quotient you get when you divide by 13 can be equally divided by 11.
9471 ÷ 11 = 861

3. The quotient you get after dividing by 11 can be equally divided by 7.   **861 ÷ 7 = 123**

4. The quotient you get after you divide by 7 is your original three-digit number. **123**

Test it with a calculator. Then show it to some friends. They will be amazed.

Honey Pots

Joe Bear has 21 honey pots. Seven pots are full of honey, 7 contain no honey at all and 7 are half full.

Joe wants to divide his honey pots with his sister and brother. Each bear will receive the same number of pots and an equal amount of honey.

No honey will be poured from one pot to another. None of the bears will have 4 pots of the same kind – full, half-full or empty. How does Joe divide his honey pots? (Hint: It helps to draw a picture.)

Answers

Pages 4/5 The Friendship Star

Since each friendship star uses 4 triangles, you need to find how many groups of 4 are in 15. You can use a division problem to find the answer:

```
        3 R 3
    4) 1 5
     - 1 2
         3
```

You can make 3 stars and have 3 triangles left over.

You can find how many friendship stars are in the quilt by dividing to find how many groups of 4 are in 140.

```
        3 5
    4) 1 4 0
     - 1 2
         2 0
       - 2 0
         0 0
```

The 5-pointed star takes 5 triangles to make. Use a division problem to find out how many groups of 5 are in 140.

There are 28 with no triangles left over.

```
        2 8
    5) 1 4 0
     - 1 0
         4 0
       - 4 0
         0 0
```

6/7 Facts Five

No answers.

8 Dividing by Subtracting

Five 6's were subtracted from 30.

$36 \div 6 = 6$	$49 \div 7 = 7$	$28 \div 4 = 7$
$45 \div 5 = 9$	$36 \div 9 = 4$	$46 \div 7 = 6R4$
$36 \div 4 = 9$	$49 \div 8 = 6R1$	$35 \div 5 = 7$
$75 \div 6 = 12R3$	$95 \div 5 = 19$	$37 \div 4 = 9R1$

$27 \div 3 = 9$	$64 \div 8 = 8$
$54 \div 6 = 9$	$72 \div 9 = 8$
$63 \div 9 = 7$	$58 \div 7 = 8R2$
$57 \div 9 = 6R3$	$49 \div 5 = 9R4$

9 Dividing by 9's and 3's

765 (9,3)   267 (3)   376 (neither)

558 (9,3)   2,126 (neither)   1,362 (3)

4,063 (neither)   1,125 (9,3)

11,574 (9,3)   59,239 (neither)

2,886 (3)   22,359 (3)

27

Answers

10 Beanstalk Race

$14 \div 7 = 2$ $20 \div 5 = 4$
$43 \div 6 = 7R1$ $64 \div 9 = 7R1$
$14 \div 3 = 4R2$ $27 \div 8 = 3R3$

$36 \div 6 = 6$ $16 \div 2 = 8$
$74 \div 8 = 9R2$ $83 \div 9 = 8R2$
$48 \div 9 = 5R3$ $59 \div 7 = 8R3$

$55 \div 9 = 6R1$ $24 \div 7 = 3R3$
$33 \div 4 = 8R1$ $50 \div 8 = 6R2$
$19 \div 4 = 4R3$ $20 \div 3 = 6R2$

11 Cross Numbers

¹2	²3	³3	⁴1	⁵5	⁶1
⁷3	⁸2	⁹5	¹⁰7	¹¹2	5
	¹²9	¹³1	¹⁴4	¹⁵2	
		¹⁶7	¹⁷6	¹⁸8	¹⁹6
²⁰2	²¹3		²²1 ²³2		²⁴8 2
	²⁵8	²⁶3	²⁷3 ²⁸2		
		2		²⁹1 3	2

12 Remainder Riddle

3 ÷ 2	5 ÷ 2	7 ÷ 2	8 ÷ 2	11 ÷ 2	13 ÷ 2	15 ÷ 2
17 ÷ 2	18 ÷ 2	3 ÷ 3	6 ÷ 3	11 ÷ 3	12 ÷ 3	17 ÷ 3
19 ÷ 3	21 ÷ 3	24 ÷ 3	27 ÷ 3	6 ÷ 4	9 ÷ 4	14 ÷ 4
18 ÷ 4	20 ÷ 4	24 ÷ 4	28 ÷ 4	33 ÷ 4	36 ÷ 4	7 ÷ 5
13 ÷ 5	16 ÷ 5	22 ÷ 5	25 ÷ 5	31 ÷ 5	35 ÷ 5	42 ÷ 5
45 ÷ 5	6 ÷ 6	15 ÷ 6	19 ÷ 6	28 ÷ 6	30 ÷ 6	36 ÷ 6
42 ÷ 6	48 ÷ 6	56 ÷ 6	9 ÷ 7	17 ÷ 7	21 ÷ 7	28 ÷ 7
35 ÷ 7	42 ÷ 7	49 ÷ 7	59 ÷ 7	63 ÷ 7	8 ÷ 8	16 ÷ 8
24 ÷ 8	32 ÷ 8	40 ÷ 8	49 ÷ 8	56 ÷ 8	64 ÷ 8	72 ÷ 8
18 ÷ 9	27 ÷ 9	36 ÷ 9	57 ÷ 9	63 ÷ 9	72 ÷ 9	81 ÷ 9

13 Mystery Square

This is what your mystery square should look like when it's finished:

4	9	2
3	5	7
8	1	6

The secret is that the sum of each row, column and diagonal is equal to 15. Here are the answers to the division problems:

$$12 \overline{)52} = 4\ R4 \qquad 10 \overline{)69} = 6\ R9 \qquad 17 \overline{)53} = 3\ R2$$

$$19 \overline{)79} = 4\ R3 \qquad 13 \overline{)96} = 7\ R5 \qquad 15 \overline{)157} = 10\ R7$$

$$18 \overline{)116} = 6\ R8 \qquad 22 \overline{)441} = 20\ R1 \qquad 11 \overline{)358} = 32\ R6$$

14/15 Greatest Quotient Game

The answer to the division problem on the game board is 62.

The secret to getting a larger quotient is to make the divisor smaller or the dividend larger.

16 The Path of No Remainders

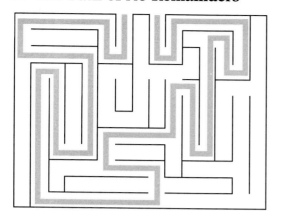

17 Missing Numbers Puzzles

$$4)\overline{96} = 24, \quad 8, \quad 16, \quad 16, \quad 0$$
$$3)\overline{87} = 29, \quad 6, \quad 27, \quad 27, \quad 0$$
$$6)\overline{84} = 14, \quad 6, \quad 24, \quad 24, \quad 0$$
$$7)\overline{91} = 13, \quad 7, \quad 21, \quad 21, \quad 0$$

$$12)\overline{398} = 33, \quad 36, \quad 38, \quad 36, \quad 2$$
$$5)\overline{685} = 137, \quad 5, \quad 18, \quad 15, \quad 35, \quad 35, \quad 0$$
$$7)\overline{959} = 137, \quad 7, \quad 25, \quad 21, \quad 49, \quad 49, \quad 0$$

18/19 Pyramid Puzzles

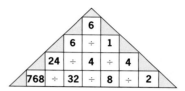

20/21 A Visit to an Enchanted Forest

No answers.

22/23 Division Decoder

DECODER						
A	**B**	**C**	**D**	**E**	**F**	**G**
20 R1	2 R3	2 R6	1 R10	2 R4	6 R2	4 R3
H	**I**	**J**	**K**	**L**	**M**	**N**
3 R2	2 R5	81 R1	31 R2	52 R2	81 R4	90 R8
O	**P**	**Q**	**R**	**S**	**T**	**U**
33 R1	72 R3	51 R5	75 R1	72 R5	11 R7	21 R5
V	**W**	**X**	**Y**	**Z**		
10 R5	22 R10	31 R7	9 R8	15 R2		

Answers

What is hard to beat?

A hard-boiled egg.

What kind of insect goes skin diving?

A mosquito.

What animal keeps the best time?

A watchdog.

How can a piece of wood become a king?

By being made into a ruler.

How can you fall off a ladder without getting hurt?

Fall from the bottom rung.

What happens when a cat eats a lemon?

It becomes a sour puss.

24 Dividing with Mayan Numbers

15 ÷ 3 = —   50 ÷ 5 = =

18 ÷ 6 = • • •   64 ÷ 8 = •••‾

24 ÷ 4 = •‾

25 More Riddles and Games

180 ÷ 30 = 6 (no noughts); 800 ÷ 20 = 40 (one nought); 2,800 ÷ 40 = 70 (one nought); 6,000 ÷ 50 = 120 (one nought); 9,000 ÷ 30 = 300 (two noughts); 800 ÷ 400 = 2 (no noughts); 16,000 ÷ 800 = 20 (one nought); 40,000 ÷ 80 = 500 (two noughts); 240,000 ÷ 60 = 4,000 (three noughts)

Kim will get 10 free bags in all. This is how. She will get 8 free bags with the 71 labels and have 7 labels left over. Each of the 8 free bags has a label so she uses them to get her ninth free bag. With the ninth bag's labels and the 7 labels she had left over at the beginning, Kim can get her tenth bag.

Each person received 1 orange because one of the mothers was the daughter of the other, making a total of three people only.

26 Three-Digit Number Puzzle.

No answers.

Honey Pots:

	Full	Half-full	Empty
Joe	3	1	3
brother	2	3	2
sister	2	3	2

Glossary

column An up-and-down arrangement of things.

diagonal A line connecting opposite corners of a shape.

example: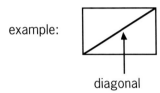

diagonal

digits The symbols used to write numerals: 0, 1, 2, 3, 4, 5, 6, 7, 8 and 9.

dividend The number that is divided in a division problem.

$$\frac{4}{6)24} \leftarrow \text{dividend}$$

division A mathematical operation with two numbers that results in a quotient.

divisor The number by which a dividend is divided.

$$\text{divisor} \rightarrow \frac{4}{6)24}$$

quotient The answer to a division problem (other than the remainder).

$$\frac{4}{6)27} \leftarrow \text{quotient}$$
$$-24$$
$$3$$

remainder The number left over in a division problem. The remainder must be less than the divisor.

$$\frac{4}{6)27}$$
$$-24$$
$$3 \leftarrow \text{remainder}$$

row A number of objects arranged in a straight line.

sum The number obtained by adding two or more numbers together.

triangle A shape with three straight sides.

31

Index